D1445178

Cover *An Afghan patrol in the Panjshir Valley*

Frontispiece *Afghan rebels testing a weapon captured from the Soviet enemy*

THE
CONFLICT
IN
AFGHANISTAN

John C Griffiths

ROURKE ENTERPRISES INC.
Vero Beach, Florida 32964

Manufactured in England

Library of Congress Cataloging in Publication Data
Griffiths, John Charles.
    The conflict in Afghanistan/John C. Griffiths.
        p.   cm.—(Flashpoints)
    British ed. published: Hove, East Sussex, England:
    Wayland, 1987.
    Bibliography: p.
    Includes index.
    Summary: Discusses the origins, events, conclusion,
    and aftermath of the conflict in Afghanistan following
    the invasion by the Soviets.
    ISBN 0-86592-039-7
    1. Afghanistan—History—Soviet Occupation,
    1979–   —Juvenile literature.   [1. Afghanistan—
    History—Soviet Occupation, 1979–]
    I. Title.   II. Series: Flashpoints (Vero Beach, Fla.)
    DS371.2.G75   1989
    958′.1044—dc19   88-2452   CIP   AC

Contents

1
Invasion!

On December 27, 1979, as the people of the Western world were still recovering from their Christmas celebrations, they were astonished to have the usual yuletide banalities of festive television interrupted by the news of the Russian invasion of Afghanistan. Even before the news was broadcast, the movement of Russian forces across the border had already been completed in one of the most logistically brilliant military operations of the twentieth century. Ten days earlier, special units of the Soviet forces had seized important Afghan airfields, taken over the ports on the Oxus River, and occupied bridges and other key points. Within hours, they had been quickly supported by the crack troops of the 4th and 105th Airborne Divisions. In less than a week, some 120,000 troops, with all their armor, artillery and air support, had crossed the Oxus. By December 26, virtually

every strategic town and city, road and river, airport and military base was in Soviet hands, just before the winter snows so hampered any movement as to make the initial opposition negligible.

In the West, the speed of the invasion, and the relative calm that followed it in Afghanistan itself, seemed to make any practical action irrelevant as well as highly dangerous. There were the usual protests in the United Nations and trade embargoes were placed briefly on certain goods. The Americans, although militarily unwilling to confront the Soviets directly over the issue, decided instead to boycott the Olympics, which were to be held in Moscow the following summer. But for all those directly involved in Afghanistan itself, the invasion was a fait accompli about which nothing could be done.

Two views: one conflict

In the early months of the invasion, a typical young Russian conscript would undoubtedly have believed the reasons given to him by the political commissar of his regiment to justify the military intervention in Afghanistan: namely, that he was coming to the aid of a friendly and popular Marxist government that had suddenly been confronted by an American-inspired uprising by bandit elements. Nor

The Soviets have suffered heavy casualties during the bitter campaign. Here, Afghan guerrillas swarm over an enemy helicopter-gunship they have gunned down.

would he have doubted the horrific tales, well-documented and photographed, of the tortures that had been carried out on prisoners by these same bandits and of their mutilation of the dead. His successor, seven years later, would have no illusions. Sullen scowls now met him on every face in every town and village through which he passed; three-quarters of the Afghan armed services he had come to support had deserted to the enemy; the Afghan government

had only been protected from the anger of the governed by rings of Soviet troops and tanks; and, as the war dragged on, a steady stream of coffins and cripples returning to the Soviet Union revealed just how costly was the cause for which he reluctantly fought.

In 1979, his Afghan counterpart might well have been younger, for even boys are expected to bear arms in a country where to fight is to be considered a man. He would

have boasted of the prospect of death or victory, confident that his natural fighting skill and his knowledge of the terrain would prove too much for the clumsy invader. He would have expected immediate support from the West in the form of economic aid and arms, to give weight to its condemnation of the invasion. He would have firmly believed that his people would throw out the Russians, as his forebears had thrown out the British.

But seven years of fighting since the invasion would have made him realize that his enemy was more ruthless than any that his people had known; ready to kill children with booby-trapped toys; ready to burn and shoot villagers—men and women—wherever guerrillas had passed; ready to destroy crops and flatten homes in an effort to starve the population into surrender if necessary. He would have slowly realized that words were cheaper than weapons in the West and that his people would have to depend largely upon themselves. But even if victory was no longer a credible goal, he would still be a member of the Mujehadeen, a soldier of God, for whom death held only the promise of glory if he could but take at least one invading infidel with him.

To understand what motivates the Afghan freedom-fighter in his desperate situation and why the reluctant and fearful Russian conscript still confronts him, it is necessary to understand the history—social, political and economic—of a country that has been called "the fulcrum of empires."

Above *The deserted village of Domgon, in Kunar province, lies devastated after repeated attacks by Soviet planes and helicopters.*

Opposite *A determined young member of the Mujehadeen on patrol.*

15

2
A divided land

Opposite *A view typical of the contrasts in the Afghan landscape: the Bamian Valley, fringed by the Koh-i-Baba range of mountains beyond.*

Tribal tensions

The country of the Afghans is one of sharp contrasts in climate, terrain and people. It abounds in deserts of every kind, in the midst of which the traveler comes with eye-catching suddenness on green and fertile valleys, or a confetti of purple flowers scattered across seemingly arid soil. In summer, the traveler may encounter a heat that seems to make the very flesh singe, while in winter a scimitar wind guards the snow-blocked passes of the mountains that cover so much of the country.

The people vary greatly in stature, color, race and feature. This ethnic variety is the result of at least two thousand years of successive invasions, which have brought many

Below *This relief map shows the extent to which Afghanistan is covered with rugged mountain ranges.*

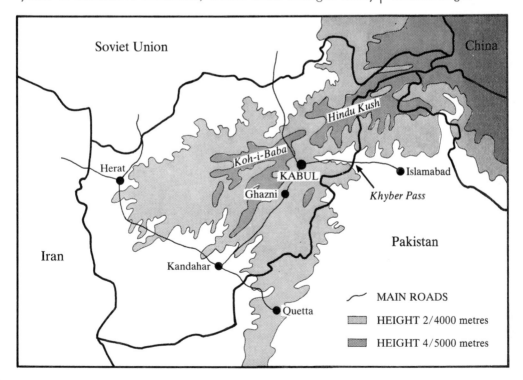

MAIN ROADS

HEIGHT 2/4000 metres

HEIGHT 4/5000 metres

17

peoples across the Hindu Kush mountains on their way toward India. The Hindu Kush cuts Afghanistan virtually in half, running from the thin strip of inaccessible mountains to the northeast that barely separates Russia, China and Pakistan, almost to the empty desert sands of the western border with Iran. To the south and southeast of the Hindu Kush lie Kandahar, Ghazni and Kabul, to the north Faizabad and Mazari-i-Sharif, and to the west Herat. Northward of these towns, the Oxus River forms the greater part of the border with Russia.

In the south of the country, the people are mainly Pathans; in the north Tajiks, Turkmen, Kirghiz and Uzbegs predominate; in the central mountains the inhabitants are mostly Hazaras. As you can appreciate from even this brief description, Afghanistan is a country divided both geographically and tribally. About half the population is made up of the Pathan tribes, which have at all times dominated the government, the civil service and the armed forces, to the virtual exclusion of other tribal groups. The Uzbegs, Hazaras, Aimaq and Nuristani (who each number about one million), the two million nomads and the numerous other small tribal groups deeply resented the fact that Afghanistan was controlled by Pathans and was consequently always preoccupied with Pathan issues. The most important of these issues was the long-running dispute with Pakistan concerning the formation of a Pathan state that would incorporate Pakistan's northwest frontier territories, where the Pathans were also in the majority.

The British, in defining the frontier between Pakistan and Afghanistan during the nineteenth century (see page 32), had tried to ensure that various Pathan tribes in both countries were grouped so that their market towns lay on the appropriate side of the border. Despite the fact that there are few enmities more fierce than those between some of the Pathan tribes, their people on both sides of the border had a common language and common ethnic origins and this provided a useful political excuse for those rulers of Afghanistan with ambitions for expansion. The arguments and, indeed, the armed clashes that these claims provoked, provided a constant source of friction between Afghanistan and Pakistan. They also offered the Soviet Union many opportunities to exploit Afghanistan's need for alternative outlets for its goods when, during the course of such disputes, Pakistan would close its borders. One might have thought

Opposite A group of Orakzai, a Pathan tribe of the Afghan-Indian frontier region. During the Afghan wars, the tribe gained a reputation among their British opponents for being fierce and uncompromising.

Opposite *This Mujehadeen outpost above Puzhgur, in Panjshir, is manned principally by Uzbeg tribesmen, here seen firing upon an Afghan army unit.*

that the smaller non-Pathan tribes would therefore have welcomed and supported a Marxist coup and even a Soviet occupation in the hope of fairer representation, but although the minorities increased their representation significantly in Babrak Karmal's first government (formed in 1979), resistance to the Russians has been as vigorous in their territories as elsewhere.

Islam and the collective spirit

Despite these intertribal tensions, the collective spirit of the Afghans is not easily shaken, as the Soviets have found to their cost since the invasion. Resistance has been vigorous and uniform across the country in all tribal territories. The vast majority of the people accept and believe in Islam in a form virtually unchanged since the days when their forefathers were converted by force in the tenth century A.D. The practices of Islam are deeply rooted in everyday life and, in the days before the Soviet invasion, some fifteen thousand mosques provided thriving centers of both religion and education. The doctrines that are followed are those of the Sunni persuasion, with its strict belief in the literal interpretation of the Koran, thus confirming a traditional lifestyle resistant to change. So strict are these practices

Below *The Islamic faith provides a strong, collective bond for the Mujehadeen, some of whom are seen here at prayer with their weapons by their sides.*

21

Mujehadeen members raise Soviet Kalishnikov rifles, captured in battle.

that the Shia doctrines of neighboring Iran (and of their own Hasara people) are despised by most Afghans. It is clear that Islam provides a center of stability, a unifying factor for the many ethnic groups that otherwise would have little in common. In the face of the invasion, tribal differences have been submerged under the overriding cause of the Mujehadeen, the soldiers of Islam, who would gladly die to defend their faith. Whether this idealistic, some would say reactionary, faith is an intellectual barrier to Marxist materialism may be open to debate, but the almost fanatical zeal it gives its adherents to throw out the unbelieving invaders, even at the cost of their own lives, cannot be doubted.

This traditional stability provided by Islam has been important in a country that was nominally a kingdom, but in which the monarch possessed little effective power or influence. Although twenty-five dynasties ruled over the country, including those of Asoka, Genghis Khan, Timur (Tamburlaine) and Babur (the Great Mogul), the vast majority of them simply imposed a degree of military rule over a myriad patchwork of tiny conflicting groups, tribes and communities. As a result of this diversity and the daunting problems of communication, the country was seldom controlled by a strong, centralized government—unlike Iran, the country's most powerful neighbor to the west. Afghanistan remained a collection of virtually autonomous

Some fifty Afghan tribal leaders, representing a dozen tribes, gather to plan their strategy in the guerrilla war against the Soviet invaders.

towns and regions, each of which ruled itself by means of a local council, or *Jirgah*, led by mullahs, landowners and village elders, but in which every adult male could have his say.

The Afghan, and the Pathan in particular, has a remarkable capacity for combining exaggerated individuality with the ability to cooperate on a commonly agreed objective with other members of his community. The Pathan, however poor, regards no man as his superior, and anyone outside his tribal group as definitely inferior. Every few generations, a leader will arrive who combines the traditional ideal qualities of the warrior-poet and he will briefly command allegiance beyond the borders of his tribe. It is this combination of almost contradictory qualities that make the Afghans unbeatable as individuals or as guerrilla groups, and almost unmanageable as anything larger.

A typical Afghan village, small and close-knit, with its terraced fields.

Economy and social structure

About 15 to 20 percent of Afghanistan's population is nomadic, but the majority of its people depend on agriculture or its associated trades for their livelihood. Over half the land is owned by individual males, but the average size of plot that they cultivate is only seven acres. There is still very little industrial development in the country and, until the exploitation of natural gas in the north to supply the Soviet Union, the largest legal exports were cotton, dried fruit and Karakul (Persian lamb) skins. Large-scale smuggling, principally in timber and highly profitable opium, is conducted across the border with Pakistan. This traffic still continues in spite of the war, indeed it has become a vital part of the efforts to raise cash to buy weapons.

The rather primitive economic pattern that exists in Afghanistan is scarcely surprising in a country where four-fifths of the land is either desert, in the form of massive

The Kabul–Jalalabad highway, which was funded and built with Soviet assistance, snakes its way through the Hindu Kush mountains.

25

mountain ranges towering up to 20,000 feet (6,100m) or low plains and plateaus of sand and rock, where temperatures can rise to well over 122°F (50°C). The impenetrability of such terrain left large tracts of the country so isolated that the wheel was virtually unknown in most villages as recently as thirty years ago. Since then, however, a great deal of progress has been made in internal transportation systems, with a trunk route connecting all the main cities. But the purpose of these new roads, whose construction began under Soviet aid and supervision in the mid-1950s, was military rather than commercial. Ultimately, the roads served only to facilitate the Soviet invasion and occupation of the country rather than to improve its internal communications and economy.

Various reforms were attempted in the 1970s, but they did little to advance the prosperity of the ordinary citizen. In 1977, the average individual annual income in the country was 120 dollars, with between 20 to 40 percent of the population falling below the United Nation's definition of the poverty line. Yet, despite this, the more obvious signs of disease and malnutrition, or indeed discontentment, were far less apparent in Afghanistan than in many other Asian states that were, according to the statisticians, far more prosperous.

Agricultural methods in Afghanistan have remained virtually unchanged for centuries. Here, the harvest is threshed by hand and with oxen.

In 1977, the last year for which even remotely reliable statistics are available, the population of Afghanistan was approximately fifteen million. The provision of health services in the country was scant, with an average of one doctor to every 13,000 people. The majority of these doctors were concentrated in the capital, Kabul, where the ratio of doctor to patients was 1 to 1,000. In some of the more remote areas of the country, however, this ratio was as high as 1 to 200,000—in practical terms, nonexistent.

An almost timeless scene—a marketplace by the Kabul River.

27

Education fared little better, being dominated by the traditional Islamic *Madrassah* system, under which the local mosque acts as a school, with the mullah as teacher. As a result, studies centered around the oral instruction of the Koran, with little time devoted to other matters. It is estimated that only about an eighth of the population could read or write—one man in five, but only one woman in twenty-five—and very few people over the age of forty were literate. Eighty percent of the population as a whole had

Young Afghan boys learn to recite the Koran under the supervision of a mullah.

received no formal schooling, women being the worst sufferers. Some advances were being made, however, as is suggested by the fact that by that time something like half the number of ten-year-old boys had attended school, and even the 5 to 10 percent of girls who had done so reflected an improvement on former times!

Women, who make up 55 percent of the population, are a badly underprivileged group in Afghanistan. They are largely deprived not only of educational and economic opportunities but also of the right to deal with their own property and person as they see fit—contrary, incidentally, to the basic tenets of Islam. One might have expected, therefore, that they would welcome the arrival of Soviet-backed

The underprivileged women of Afghanistan may have the most to gain from a peaceful settlement of the conflict.

29

AFGHANISTAN 1980

DOWN WITH BABRAK
THIS PUPPET OF
RUSSIAN IN
AFGHANISTAN

That Afghan women should protest openly and publicly against the Soviet invasion is indicative of the irreversible social changes that the resistance and refugee status have brought about.

socialism with its recognition of the rights of women, but they have in fact been as dedicated in their resistance to the occupying forces as their menfolk. It is an accidental by-product of the existence of the Afghan refugee camps in Pakistan, and to a lesser extent of the few in Iran (which together now hold something like a third of the whole population of Afghanistan), that they have brought about considerable advances in education, health standards and even the emancipation of women in the absence of husbands, fathers and brothers on guerrilla duties. Should the refugees ever return to their homeland, their experiences in these camps will profoundly alter the old traditional patterns of life that have remained unchanged for so long.

3
Imperialist invaders

The British in Afghanistan

As a nation state, in the modern sense, Afghanistan has existed for less than 250 years. The enmity among its races, and within the tribes of these races themselves, has only been contained during that time by the converging pressures of the Russian and British empires. Throughout the nineteenth century, the country found itself the subject of the imperialist ambitions of both these major powers. Russia wished to exploit the country's position in order to open up a reliable and profitable trade route to the oceans to

A British army camp near the Khyber Pass during the second Afghan war in 1878.

Troops prepare to fend off an Afghan attack on a British fort outside Kabul in December 1879.

the south, while Britain remained more interested in controlling the country for strategic reasons. They were initially drawn into Afghanistan in an attempt to counter the Persians, who, with Russian support, invaded the country in 1837. A friendly and stable Afghanistan was seen by Britain as a way both to check Russian imperialist ambitions and to dampen down sources of internal conflicts in India that might affect the empire's profitable trade routes.

British attitudes toward the country fluctuated depending on whether the Liberals or the Conservatives were in power. The Liberals favored the concept of using Afghanistan as a buffer state without directly interfering in its government, while the Conservatives preferred direct occupation as a means of furthering British interests. Twice during the course of the nineteenth century, the British invaded Afghanistan (1838–42; 1878–81). Twice they suffered initial military disasters before eventually defeating the tribesmen, only then to discover that though they might win military victories, they could never achieve ultimate control. The British claimed on the first occasion, as do the present Soviet invaders, that they were not invading Afghanistan but "supporting" the ruler (who happened to have been put there by the British in the first place) "against foreign interference and factious opposition." Toward the end of the first Afghan war, in January 1842, the British lost an entire army as they retreated from Kabul, some 4,500 troops, at the hands of the guerrilla tribesmen, but by the autumn they had recaptured the city. During the campaign, one British major-general ordered that every man, woman and child within the village of Killah-Chuk should be butchered in revenge for the wiping out of a detachment of his men. In due course, recognizing the impracticability of occupying Afghanistan, the British withdrew their armies. This pattern of invasion and withdrawal was to be repeated twice more before an exhausted Britain, its imperial will and power wavering, finally disengaged itself from the country after the brief, third Afghan war in 1919.

Russian expansionism

During the second half of the nineteenth century, the Russians moved inexorably southward into central Asia. They captured the cities of Bukhara, Samarkand and Tashkent, establishing strong and effective rule over what are now the provinces of Soviet Turkmenistan and Uzbekistan.

In addition, the tribes of the Steppes—the Kirghiz, Uzbegs and Turkmen, whose kinsmen can now be found in large numbers on the Afghan side of the border—had been steadily conquered as part of a general Russian policy of economic and territorial expansion. This involved expanding to the west through the Balkans, as well as to the south.

In 1885, the Russians defeated an Afghan army barring their final advance to the Oxus River. Shortly afterward, it was made quite clear in the Russian newspaper *Novosti*, which spoke for the Russian government, that this conquest did not mark the end of Russian ambitions in the area. The Afghan city of Herat lay within easy grasp, and *Novosti* urged that Russia must press on to occupy it and so "pierce a window looking southeastward, a convenient halting place for a still farther advance toward the Indian Ocean, in fulfillment of Russia's historic destiny."

Throughout the nineteenth century, the obsession of the landlocked Russian empire, whose few seaports were frozen up for much of the year, was to acquire a warm-water port. The most obvious and accessible of such ports lay in those parts of the British empire that are now part of Pakistan. However, at this time, Britain was the undisputed world superpower, and its occasional forays into Afghanistan and Persia were sufficient to check Russian imperial ambitions. In 1856 (through the "Peace of Paris" treaty) and 1878 (at the Congress of Berlin), the Russians had to accept humiliating terms to settle disputes with other major powers in the area. They remained inhibited from further attack, in military terms at least, until the 1979 invasion. Indeed, it was not until after World War II that the Soviet Union exercised any significant direct influence over Afghanistan's internal affairs.

An Afridi picket near a British fort at Jumrood in 1879.

Independence and civil strife

The early years of the twentieth century saw the major powers turn their attention away from the East, concentrating instead on the struggle for power going on in Europe. The rise of German European imperialism, the communist revolution in Russia, and the steady decline of the power and influence of the British empire, allowed Afghanistan to enjoy a period of relative freedom from the external pressures applied by Britain and, to a lesser extent, Russia. In 1919, King Amanullah, who had seized the throne following the murder of his father, saw the opportunity to free his country from outside interference and declared his country's independence in internal and external affairs. This move precipitated the third Afghan war with an unenthusiastic and war-weary Britain and, after only a few months, King Amanullah won a peace treaty that recognized his country's independence.

Russian troops advance on the Afghans at Pul-i-Kuisti, in 1885.

Unfortunately, Amanullah allowed his passionate desire to introduce Western reforms, such as the abolition of *purdah*, to sweep aside the caution necessary for making progress in such an essentially conservative society. The mullahs rose in revolt, Amanullah abdicated and, in January 1929, the throne was held for nine months by a flamboyant brigand known as Bachai i Saqao—"son of the water carrier." However, Nadir Shah, Amanullah's cousin, was able to seize control of power thanks to the crucial allegiance of most of the Pathans on both sides of the border. Their influence helped him to be elected king unanimously in a tribal assembly held in October 1929. Although he reigned for only four years, he quickly imposed political stability on the country, his crowning achievement being to establish a national parliament with two chambers. In addition he initiated a gradual program of economic and social change. After his death in 1933, he was succeeded by his son Mohammed Zahir, who embarked upon the type of calm and conservative administration that continued until the bloodless coup that saw Mohammed Dauod take power in 1973, thus peacefully ending the system of monarchical rule in Afghanistan.

Opposite *Amanullah Khan wished to abolish the system of* purdah, *an Islamic code by which women were kept out of public view as much as possible. One requirement of this law was that women should wear a* chadira, *or veil, when in public.*

Left *Sardar Mohammed Dauod, who returned to power in 1973 following a bloodless coup.*

37

4
Hopes and failures (1963–79)

In the thirty years immediately following World War II, the West, and the United States in particular, was preoccupied with affairs in other areas of the world, and Afghanistan was left largely neglected. The Soviet Union took advantage of this indifference to achieve a high degree of economic penetration through "aid" projects, which made the Afghan economy virtually dependent on the Soviet Union. By the late 1970s, the Soviets had also gained a key role in equipping, training and "advising" the Afghan armed forces.

This growth of Soviet influence in the country showed that although their ambitions had changed in kind, they had not been deflected entirely in direction. In 1919 Leon Trotsky wrote "the road to Paris and London lies through the towns of Afghanistan, the Punjab and Bengal." Twenty-one years later, the Soviet Foreign Minister, Molotov, made it clear during negotiations with the Nazis that "the area south of Batum and Baku in the general direction of the Persian Gulf is . . . the center of the aspirations of the Soviet Union." Economic and military assistance provided the perfect means to achieve these goals without having to take the risk of an invasion. Afghanistan, while remaining independent, could slowly be converted into a Soviet satellite country.

In 1963, Prince Dauod, who had effectively ruled Afghanistan for a decade, was pressed into standing down so that democratic government could be introduced. The royal family barred themselves from direct government by the new constitution. Secret ballot elections were held for the 216 seats in the *Wolasi Jirgah*, or lower house, and for two-thirds of the 84 seats in the *Meshrano Jirgah*, the upper house, the rest of whose members were appointed by the king.

There were no fewer than 1,358 candidates in the first general election for the *Wolasi Jirgah* seats in 1965. The

Opposite *One of the most spectacular projects undertaken in the 1960s with Soviet aid was the construction of this hydroelectric power station near Kabul.*

The Wolasi Jirgah, *or lower house of parliament, in session during the brief period of democratic rule.*

Opposite *The economic and social reforms of the 1960s meant that the country's major cities, particularly Kabul, underwent some modernization. However, life outside these areas remained largely unaffected.*

campaign itself was free from interference. But even in the cities only 5 to 10 percent of the electorate actually voted and, in the rural areas, the figure was as low as 2 percent, so that the members of the first Afghan parliament were hardly representative of the people in the Western sense.

Subsequent election turnouts showed little improvement. This was not only due to the natural suspicion held by Afghans for all forms of state activity, though this was probably the most significant factor, but also because it was increasingly clear that the system was not working. The legislature, the two houses of parliament, was still powerless in the face of the executive, those who held the key government positions. Many ministers were not even members of the *Jirgahs*, and the king tended to use his power of appointment of the prime minister whenever things weren't going as he would have liked. A decade later, when the experiment had palpably failed because of the lack of courage and commitment of those who had launched it, Dauod seized power again in a military coup—the traditional path to power in Afghanistan.

Dauod was dubbed "the Red Premier" in the West because of the growing Soviet influence over the country's economy, but by the mid-1970s he was already showing that he was much more a patriot than a Marxist and began to loosen the economic ties with his northern neighbor. To protect his own position, he dispersed many of the young

men of the two tiny Marxist groups in the country (*Khalq* and *Parcham*) to the more remote and resolutely Muslim parts of Afghanistan. He began to purge Marxists from key military posts and promised new legislative elections that would have brought back substantial conservative elements into government. But when he began to assert Afghan independence of the Soviet Union in foreign policy—in condemning their use of Cuban troops in Angola, for example—his days were numbered. Dauod sometimes claimed that he staged his coup because he was impatient with Afghanistan's slow progress toward becoming a modern state under a democratic regime. Could the Marxists who overthrew him in 1978, a faction representing only a very small minority of the population, reasonably have claimed an equally justifiable impatience?

Afghan soldiers leave an army base during the coup of 1978.

The rise and fall of the PDP (1978–79)

Dauod's coup had been popular and bloodless. The one that toppled him in April 1978, almost certainly engineered by the KGB, who had an operational unit in Afghanistan at the time, was the reverse. Although it was Nur Mohammed Taraki—civilized and not unpopular, but a theoretician—who became premier, it was one of his two lieutenants, Hafizullah Amin, who was clearly the man who wielded practical power.

The coup that brought the People's Democratic Party (PDP) to power in 1978 came about because of impatience among left-wing intellectuals with the slow progress of social, political and economic modernization under Dauod. The fighting that occurred during the week that it took for the coup to be completed was fierce, but limited to clashes between loyalist and communist factions within the armed forces, while the people themselves did not take to the streets.

Although it had recruited successfully in colleges and in the armed forces, the PDP's membership at the time of the coup was a mere 6,000 people in a nation of some 15 million. Most of these lived in Kabul, the country's only major city.

Nur Mohammed Taraki, joint leader of the People's Democratic Party (PDP), who became prime minister in April 1978.

The party, therefore, was largely insensitive to the traditions and living conditions in the villages, where 90 percent of the population lived. In addition, PDP members had received only a limited education in socialist principles, usually gleaned from a handful of pamphlets that had been translated into Persian and supplied by Moscow. Feroz Ahmed, a leading socialist in neighboring Pakistan, expressed great disappointment in the state of PDP at the time of the revolution. "There has been very little indigenous work," he said, "a real dearth of analyses of the concrete political situation in Afghanistan. This party did not know about its own rural society." Even its limited membership was split into rival factions—*Khalq*, regarded as more hardline Marxists and led by Taraki, and *Parcham*, more moderate and led by Babrak Karmal.

Hafizullah Amin, who succeeded Taraki in September 1979, following the latter's death in a gun battle at the Soviet Embassy.

General Alexei Yepishev, a member of the Soviet Commission for Foreign Affairs, who was sent to assess the political situation in Afghanistan in March 1979.

The PDP were determined to bring about rapid reforms in the nation's economy in an attempt to make it more modern and efficient along Socialist lines. However, their basic lack of understanding of the country's rural traditions and attitudes meant that their efforts soon met with opposition. Instead of modifying their policies, they applied them with greater and greater brutality. "Torture," said Abdul Ghafur, former chief of administration for the Afghan Ministry of the Interior in the months following the PDP-led coup, "was simply the mood of the day. Everyone was

suspected of leading a countercoup." As resistance grew, the government began to take military action. Dissidents were shot or imprisoned and, by March 1979, a civil war was already well under way. At Herat, near the Iranian frontier, thousands of civilians and members of the armed forces rose up against the government. Much of the city was bombed by air force planes, perhaps manned by Soviet pilots. Five thousand people were killed and wounded before the uprising was crushed. In one of the many attacks on government officials in Herat, several Soviet advisers were flayed alive. The Soviet Union sent General Yepishev, the man who had masterminded the invasion of Czechoslovakia in 1968, to assess the situation. The Soviet Union had, by and large, discouraged the implementation of too rapid reforms by the PDP. It may have hoped gradually to build up widespread popular support for the regime through its economic aid programs.

Soon, Amin replaced Taraki as premier, though for the time being Taraki remained titular head of state. In September 1979, in a gangster-style shootout at the Soviet Embassy, which had probably been intended to remove the increasingly unpopular Amin, it was Taraki who was killed and Amin took total power. The Russians made the best of a bad job and recognized the new leader, but, seeing that his tyrannical regime was too unpopular to govern unassisted, they sent their combat troops into Afghanistan in significant numbers for the first time. These consisted of special armed units whose role in any Soviet invasion plan was to seize and hold key points, such as airfields, pending the arrival of the main invasion force.

By December, so many Afghans were fighting the regime that the Christmas Eve invasion had become inevitable. The Afghan army was losing the war on all fronts, with thousands of soldiers deserting to join the Mujehadeen. Amin's regime was on the point of collapse in the face of such widespread armed resistance and, in response to his appeal for help, Soviet airborne troops invaded. Within a week, Afghanistan was occupied by over 100,000 Soviet troops. It was the last success the Russians were to enjoy. Whether by accident or design, Amin was killed during the confusion of the invasion. The Russians announced on December 27 that they had executed him in the hope of winning support for their new protégé, Babrak Karmal, whom they installed in his place.

Opposite *Babrak Karmal meets Leonid Brezhnev, the late Soviet leader, in December 1981.*

5
The Soviet intervention

The strike force

The pattern of the Soviet invasion is interesting to analyze. Once the key airfields of Begram and Kabul had been secured by the advance units in late autumn, the invasion was spearheaded by the elite of the Soviet armed forces—the Airborne Divisions. These seven divisions (a division equals three regiments, each made up of three battalions consisting of about four to five hundred men) are the best-trained, best-paid and best-equipped soldiers in the Soviet Union. Indeed it was the equipment that they used, the *ASU 85* armored infantry fighting vehicle and the new *AKS 74* automatic rifle, that betrayed their identity. The 4th and 105th Airborne Divisions were probably involved, though regiments from other divisions may have been included to "blood" a good cross section of soldiers in action.

These Airborne Divisions do not come under any army command, but answer directly to the Politburo. A fairly large proportion of their ranks is made up of regular soldiers (in contrast to the rest of the army, which consists almost entirely of conscripts) and members of the Communist Party, thus making them the obvious choice to deal with politically sensitive tasks. They are also almost all Greater (i.e. European) Russians, unlike other units of the Soviet army where, right down to company level, the races are deliberately mixed. The backup troops, numbering some 80,000 by the beginning of March 1980, were probably of this mixed nature. However, such is the flexibility of the Soviet army that there may have been an initial preponderance of troops from the Asiatic republics—many of whom were reported to have been replaced by non-Asian troops by that time.

The main army invaded almost entirely through the long-prepared Kushka–Herat highway and through the Kunduz–Kabul road. The Russian advisers were able to neutralize many of the units to which they were attached and, for the first time, an Afghan coup was carried out entirely by

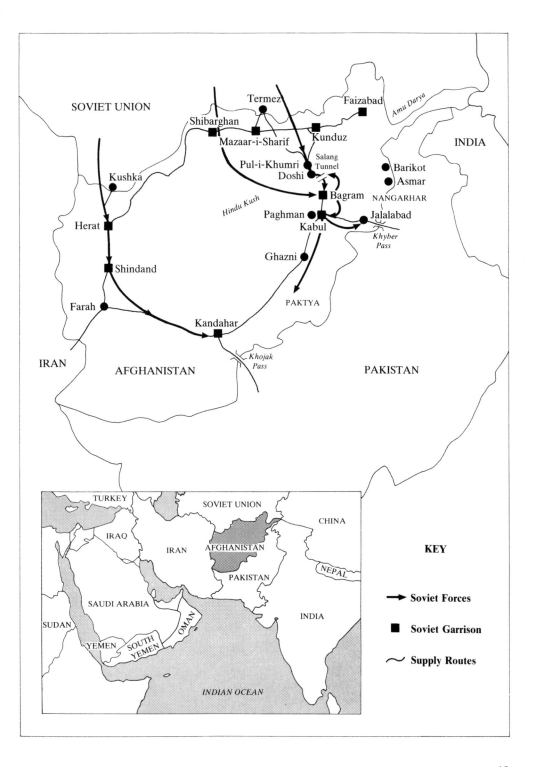

Opposite *This picture, taken from a passing car, shows a large division of Soviet troops gathered at the southern edge of Kabul airport, during the first weeks of the invasion.*

Russian troops. Unpopular as Amin was, no Afghan unit could be counted on to participate in what was virtually a foreign invasion. By the end of December, the Russians had occupied all the key towns, airfields and highways before the winter snows restricted movement and thus reduced the size and scope of possible guerrilla actions. Russian troops were therefore able to keep a low profile and were seldom engaged in direct combat with the Afghans, except in dealing with rebellious units of the Afghan army, or when Afghan troops faced certain defeat at the hands of the resistance forces, as they did at Faizabad in January 1980. Soviet-piloted helicopter gunships and *MiG 21*s, on the other hand, carried out many strikes, though the majority of air attacks were flown by Soviet-trained Afghan pilots. Until the summer of 1980, Russian forces could have disengaged from military action relatively easily and quickly. Now, without some negotiated settlement or agreement on the part of the freedom-fighters, such a withdrawal would be fraught with military hazard.

Below *A Soviet armored vehicle rolls into Kabul during the initial invasion.*

A legitimate invasion?

The crucial question that must be asked however, is not "were the Russians legitimately invited in to the country under the defense treaty of 1978?"—arguably they were—but rather "whether the government that invited them was itself legitimate"? The two warring factions of the Afghan Marxist party, *Khalq* and *Parcham*, never attracted much support even at the height of their popularity. They came to power by a military coup—as had admittedly the government they overthrew—and were able to stay in power only by increasingly repressive measures and military force. Even then they controlled only the main cities and, as the uprisings in Herat and Kandahar had shown, these power bases themselves were tenuously held. The most damning evidence, however, against the moral legitimacy of the invasion must be the almost universal hostility and armed resistance with which the invaders were greeted. So hated were these foreigners—as their British predecessors had been—that within two years, more than two-thirds of the Afghan army and air force had deserted, many of them to join the rebels, others simply to give away their weapons before going home. Today, there is no pretence that the 120,000 Russian servicemen are there only to support and advise the Afghan forces, for theirs is now the principal military presence in the country.

Above *Anti-aircraft guns stand openly on the streets of Herat in defiance of the Soviet invaders.*

Opposite *A Soviet bomber pounds guerrilla positions in the Panjshir Valley.*

Some Soviet soldiers have become so disillusioned that they have deserted to the rebel forces. This young Russian has been converted to Islam and now leads a Mujehadeen guerrilla unit at Khanabad.

There had, of course, been strong advocates of the initial invasion among the Russian leaders, particularly those members of the Politburo who were drawn from the armed services. Soviet forces had never been involved in serious combat since World War II. As the Soviet novelist Aleksandr Porkhanov put it, "Commanders with gray on their temples found themselves under fire for the first time in the foothills of Afghanistan." Here, then, was an opportunity for the Soviet military to try out men and equipment in actual combat.

Afghan guerrillas search the bodies of Soviet troops killed during an ambush of an armored-car patrol. The Soviets have learned through bitter experience that the rebels are a tough and skillful enemy.

Among lesser considerations, no doubt, was a desire to protect the economic investment made in such projects as the Shibarghan gasfield and pipeline across the Oxus, and to secure the huge mineral reserves of copper and iron-ore in the Hajigak. However, perhaps the most significant motive of all was the recognition that to allow an Islamic tribal rebellion to overthrow a Soviet-sponsored Marxist government would set a dangerous precedent for Russia's own internal subject-peoples across the border. Turkmen, Uzbegs and Tajiks are to be found in considerable numbers on both sides of the Afghan–Soviet border, and those on the Soviet side are as devoted to Islam and to their national traditions as their Afghan kinsmen, despite fifty years of secularization and Russification. Seeing a successful rebellion, they too might have sought to throw off their master's yoke in like manner.

On the other hand, the successful consolidation of a Soviet

A Soviet repair team mend a gas pipeline damaged by Afghan guerrillas.

client-state in Afghanistan would have provided a useful springboard for Soviet expansion elsewhere. It must not be forgotten that, whatever the nature of its present government, for over two centuries Russia has been an imperial power. Under its communist regime, its strategic, active approach is political and economic, but its opportunist imperialism, covertly supporting revolutionary movements, is physical and military—whether indirectly as in Cuba or, more rarely, first-hand as in Afghanistan. A solidly pro-Soviet regime in Afghanistan could provide a number of opportunities for this imperial expansion. In Iran, the communists of the banned *Tudeh* party bide their time underground waiting for the chaos that could follow Ayatollah Khomeini's death or any severe reverses in the war with Iraq. If they could be supported from the East from Afghan territory, as well as from across the border with Russia, their chances of achieving power in Iran would be greatly improved.

The Soviets have been eager to present the appearance of a harmonious and mutually beneficial relationship with the Afghan people.

More important would be the opportunity to stir up trouble beyond Afghanistan's southern border. The Pathans, who heavily populate the frontier provinces on the Pakistan side of the border, are much involved in helping their kinsfolk to fight the Russians. An excuse to invade Pakistan might be tempting, but its military alliance with China and its military support from the United States would make this a dangerous ploy. A less risky policy would be to encourage the separatist tendencies of the Baluch in the west of Pakistan and thereby seek to establish another Soviet client-state in the region. This would bring Soviet influence, and perhaps Soviet military bases, up to the Straits of Hormuz. These stand opposite Oman and control the entrance to the Gulf, through which a rapidly diminishing, but still fairly significant, proportion of the West's oil supplies are carried. But, despite the training of a number of young Baluch in Moscow, there is little sign that this largely nomadic, but firmly Muslim, people would be willing to substitute a Marxist Afghan dominance for that of Pakistan.

Russian soldiers on patrol on the Kabul–Jalalabad highway.

None of these objectives could be attained without a friendly, or at least acquiescent, Afghanistan, and certainly not from a country in a state of rebellion. The present regime is both ideologically and morally bankrupt in the eyes of the Afghan people. Too many villages have been bombed, too many refugees driven from the country. Soviet bombing raids, designed to destroy crops and food supplies have failed to starve the population into surrender. The collective spirit among the people is probably stronger now than ever. In the face of such determined resistance, it is difficult to see how the Russians will establish the peace they would so dearly like to achieve.

A Soviet bombing raid on an Afghan village, designed to destroy its crops and starve the population into surrender.

6
A forgotten war

How has the West responded to the situation in Afghanistan, and how coherent and effective are its intentions for the future of the country and the steps taken to realize them?

The American boycott of the 1980 Olympics, together with the trade embargoes it briefly imposed on the Soviet Union, reflected a very genuine sense of outrage at the invasion of Afghanistan, but one that found little expression, other than in empty rhetoric, among other Western states. Even Britain, whose historic connections with Afghanistan were so strong, did little more than make diplomatic protests. When Germany invaded Poland in 1939, Britain responded with the guns of war; when Russia invaded Afghanistan in 1979, Britain suggested they should stop selling cheap butter to the Soviet Union. The difference in context, of course, for the U.S. even more than for Britain, was the existence of nuclear weapons and the corresponding need for the superpowers to fight their wars at second hand.

Russia's Vietnam?
A parallel is often drawn between Russia's involvement in Afghanistan and that of the United States in Vietnam. Although the analogy is false, the very differences between the two wars raise some interesting questions about the outcome of this forgotten conflict.

The Soviet Union enjoys a number of advantages denied to the Americans. Logistically, it has the benefit of a long border with Afghanistan and a transportation network that has been developed over a period of twenty years to reach from the Soviet Union into the heart of Afghanistan. In addition, the Mujehadeen are deeply divided among themselves and are reluctant to fight outside their local territories. Quite often, indeed, various guerrilla factions have fought each other because of old racial and tribal quarrels and jealousies. It is highly improbable, therefore, that the freedom-fighters will ever combine to form the size of fighting force that could drive the Russians out of large tracts of

Opposite *The Afghan team marches into the Olympic Stadium in Moscow for the 1980 games. Many countries from the West, notably the United States, staged a boycott in protest at the Soviet invasion of Afghanistan.*

60

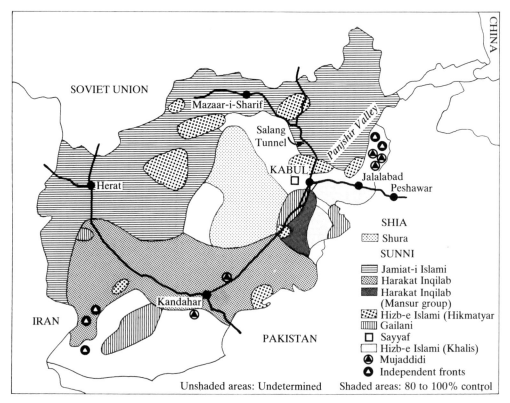

SOVIET UNION

Mazaar-i-Sharif

Salang
Tunnel

Panjshir Valley

KABUL

Herat

Jalalabad

Peshawar

CHINA

SHIA

▨ Shura

SUNNI

▤ Jamiat-i Islami

▦ Harakat Inqilab

▰ Harakat Inqilab
(Mansur group)

▨ Hizb-e Islami (Hikmatyar

▥ Gailani

☐ Sayyaf

☐ Hizb-e Islami (Khalis)

🜂 Mujaddidi

◭ Independent fronts

IRAN

Kandahar

PAKISTAN

Unshaded areas: Undetermined   Shaded areas: 80 to 100% control

Most of the Afghan resistance forces are based around the country's major cities and the Soviet supply routes.

Afghanistan permanently. Nor do the Mujehadeen receive anything like the scale of military help that was available to the Vietcong against the Americans.

On the other hand, the Soviets do face some formidable obstacles, particularly in the remarkable toughness of both the terrain and the people. For many Afghans, fighting is living, part of a centuries-old tradition to which every male child is bred and trained and which every female is expected to encourage.

Though the freedom-fighters will seldom *make* cause, they always *have* a common cause—a belief in Islam that permeates every aspect of life and sanctifies death met at the hands of a religious and national enemy. The intensity of this conviction is hard to appreciate, but very real. The guerrillas also have the advantage of the country's long, uncontrollable border with three sympathetic powers—China, Pakistan and Iran. Although they are not directly involved in the conflict, these countries provide a place of refuge, moral support and a supply route for weapons. The

Soviet Union cannot strike at these bases without risking direct confrontation with the countries concerned, or provoking a much more direct involvement by the West.

In Vietnam, the U.S. used methods of increasingly desperate ferocity the longer the campaign continued. Napalm, defoliating agents, saturation bombing and other techniques of modern warfare nevertheless proved ineffective in the face of resolute guerrilla opponents—though the Vietcong were an army in every sense by the end. The increasing reluctance

Guns and ammunition are loaded up at a camp near Telemungal. The rebels have depended heavily on such cross-border arms supplies.

A West German politician and an Afghan resistance leader demonstrate a "butterfly-bomb" and show a picture of one of its victims. The bombs are designed to attract children and to blow up when handled, causing horrific injuries.

to escalate the conflict, combined with an increasingly vociferous domestic lobby, led the Americans to disengage their forces and to desert the South Vietnamese cause. The Russians face an even more fanatically resolute, if very much less cohesive, guerrilla opposition. Equally, the mountains and deserts of Afghanistan provide even worse terrain for regular troops to attack guerrilla forces than that of the jungles of Vietnam. But the Soviet forces have outclassed the Americans in the barbarity of their methods—from toys that explode in the faces of children who pick them up, to chemical agents such as the Soma-type nerve gases banned by the Geneva Convention; from the total

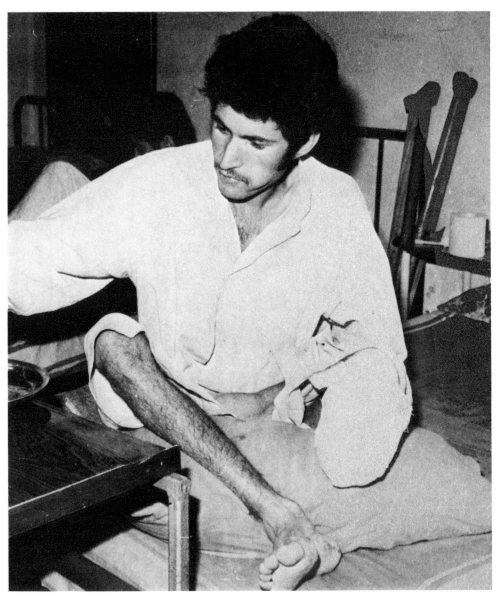

destruction of villages, crops, livestock and irrigation-systems, to the wholesale butchery of old men, women and children in villages even suspected of providing refuge, however unwillingly, to the Mujehadeen. The Soviet army and air force provide 80 percent of the government's combatants in Afghanistan and directly confront the guerrillas on a scale that was never even approached by the United States.

The dirty war. A victim of a small, Soviet anti-personnel mine that is widely used on well-known refugee routes.

Tactics and casualties

Even by the standards of conventional warfare, the tactics that have been used by the Soviets in Afghanistan have been ruthless. Some have even compared their strategy to nothing less than a form of calculated genocide. In 1986, a United Nations report drew attention to the fact that, in one year alone, some five million people had been made refugees and that 35,000 civilians had been killed. It is hard to calculate the total numbers killed in the time since the war began, but when civilians and combatants are considered together, the figure cannot be far short of half a million. Add to this the thousands who will have died, particularly the young children (the infant mortality rate is between 30 and 40 percent), through the starvation that has followed in the wake of Russia's "scorched-earth" policy and perhaps the term genocide does not seem an exaggeration. Nearly one-third of the population have been made refugees or have been killed. The astonishing thing is that today the resistance to the foreign invaders of those who remain in their country or lurk across its borders is as fierce and determined as ever.

Afghan refugees make the arduous journey across the Nangarhar Mountains to Pakistan. Nearly one-third of the population have left Afghanistan since the invasion.

But the Soviet situation differs in a respect other than its utter ruthlessness. Although the Soviet authorities find it increasingly hard to conceal the truth about the war in Afghanistan when there is scarcely a town in Russia that does not have its demobbed conscripts, its wounded veterans and grieving relatives to describe the exact nature of this colonial war, there is no organized public opinion capable of influencing the future policy of the Soviet government. It is unlikely, therefore, to suffer the loss of resolution that led to the American defeat in Vietnam. The question remains, by what means could Soviet policy be changed?

Afghan villagers return to the ruins of their homes, which have been devastated by Soviet bombing.

67

7
The future

Untying the knot

It is unlikely that any level of military losses that the Muje-hadeen could inflict would be sufficient to make the Soviet Union withdraw its forces, but a sharp increase would make this a significant influence in taking such a decision. No doubt this thought lay behind President Reagan's decision in 1986, however belated, to supply ground-to-air missiles to the resistance forces. However, much of the advantage that might have been gained by such a move was lost by making such a public issue of it.

The Soviets cannot admit to having been forced to with-draw in the face of military losses partly brought about by the Western supply of arms. The loss of face and possible implications in other satellite countries would be too serious. In this context, the Russian love of secrecy could be capitalized on to harm without being seen to harm. Moreover, any attempt to weaken the Soviet Union, by drawing it into a debilitating and protracted war, would be at the expense of the Afghans who have to do the fighting and the dying. The interests of the Afghans might best be served by helping the Soviet Union to find a plausible reason to undertake the withdrawal they now seem to desire. Within months of the Soviet invasion, there was ample evidence that they were reluctant to continue with it, an impression that has been increasingly confirmed as the fighting has become more bitter and protracted. Part of the process of reducing tension over the issue would have to be the tacit recognition that Afghanistan is quite legitimately a Soviet sphere of influence.

On July 28, 1986, Mikhail Gorbachev, the Soviet leader, announced that six regiments of troops were to be with-drawn from Afghanistan by the end of the year. He empha-sized that the move, which involved some 6,000 men, was meant "to speed up a political settlement and to give it further impetus." Since this offer, made on the eve of U.N.-sponsored talks on Afghanistan in Geneva, Gorbachev has

Opposite *Rebels triumphantly pose with a destroyed Soviet tank. Although united against their enemy, they are unable to agree on a common leader who might negotiate a peaceful settlement of the conflict.*

declared his intention to start withdrawing all Soviet troops from Afghanistan by May 1988.

Strategic calculations

With a world oil glut and the reduction in importance of the Gulf as a source of oil supplies since the Iran–Iraq war, the West can afford to be less paranoid about Soviet influence in the area. However, at the same time it will have to make a considerable political and economic investment in democratizing and stabilizing Pakistan, particularly its Baluch province. The risk here is that President Zia has sheltered and supported the Mujehadeen, while opposing and criticizing the Russians. His opponents, and principally Miss Benazir Bhutto, are leftward-inclined politically and pro-Soviet. They therefore may seek to overturn his policies for reasons of domestic popularity, despite the fact that without Pakistan's support the Afghan Mujehadeen would be doomed.

Perhaps the most difficult precondition of all that is required for a solution to the Afghan problem is to achieve sufficient cooperation among the various Mujehadeen factions for them to be able to deliver peace if they were offered it. Clearly Russia could not accept a Muslim fundamentalist, anti-Marxist, anti-Soviet regime in place of the present government, though it may have accepted that Babrak Karmal could not be part of any postwithdrawal coalition. In some respects, the West's best contribution to peace might be to become highly selective and give massive military and financial aid to one or two of the more secular and sophisticated, but nevertheless acceptably Muslim, Mujehadeen leaders—non-Pathan as well as Pathan—to help them establish the kind of leadership that could reach a just and equitable compromise with some kind of Soviet-backed Marxist group.

The difficulties are formidable and the war in Afghanistan now seems distant and overshadowed by a host of other international problems. It remains, however, one of the greatest human tragedies of the postwar era. If a peaceful solution cannot be found, of one thing we can be sure—the Afghans, of every race, will go on fighting their invaders until they have got back their country or until every last one of them is dead.

Glossary

Aimaq   One of the smaller tribes living around Herat.

Baluch   A tribe living in the most eastern part of Pakistan bordering on Iran and Afghanistan. This area is known as "the tip where Allah put the rubbish of creation."

CIA   Central Intelligence Agency, the U.S. secret service. One of its many roles is to subvert regimes disapproved of by the U.S., usually by supporting or encouraging resistance movements within the country concerned.

Flayed   A form of torture in which the skin of the victim is torn off by whipping.

Genocide   The deliberate attempt to wipe out a whole race.

Hajigak   The central mountain area of Afghanistan. It is rich in minerals, particularly copper and iron-ore.

Hazara   A people of Mongol origin who live in the Hajigak.

Hindu Kush   Literally "the killer of Hindus," the mountain range that divides Afghanistan from northeast to southwest. Before the Russians established their road and air links into the country, the Hindu Kush provided an impenetrable barrier against invading armies for most of the year.

Hormuz Straits   The narrow, 23-mile passage that separates Oman and Pakistan. It is of great strategic importance in controlling shipping to and from the Gulf.

Jirgah   Originally the name given to the council of elders that governed the traditional Pathan village, it became part of the title of the two Afghan houses of parliament— the *Wolasi Jirgah* ("peoples" or "lower" house) and the *Meshrano Jirgah* ("elders" or "upper" house).

Karakul   Persian lamb, whose soft wool is much prized in the West.

KGB   Komitet Gosudarstvenoi Bezopastnost, the Russian intelligence service that plays an equivalent role to that of the CIA.

Khalq   Literally "the masses," the name given to one of the two rival factions of the Marxist People's Democratic Party, which was responsible for the coup of 1978.

Kirghiz   The tribe living mainly in the mountainous regions of northeast Afghanistan where India, China and Pakistan meet "on the roof of the world."

Koran   The holy book of Islam.

Madrassah   A school based in a mosque where the mullah acts as teacher and where most lessons consist of learning to recite passages of the Koran from memory.

Mujehadeen   A Jehad is a holy war and the Mujehadeen are its soldiers.

Mullah   The holy man of the Islamic religion. He is more involved in secular affairs than a Western priest, combining his religious function with that of social leader, teacher and judge.

Nomads   Before the Soviet invasion there were more than two million nomads in Afghanistan, moving their goats, camels and donkeys from summer to winter pasture and back. This lifestyle, together with their role as news carriers and smugglers, has made them unpopular with the country's more bureaucratic regimes.

Parcham   Literally "the flag," the second wing of the People's Democratic Party.

Shia   The smaller of the two main sects of Islam but dominant in Iran.

Soma gas   Toxic agent that attacks the central nervous system causing convulsions, paralysis and possible death.

Sunni   The principal sect of Islam and totally dominant in Afghanistan.

Tajik   A people of Persian descent who mainly farm the areas of north Afghanistan and who are now fiercely resisting the Russian invaders.

Tudeh   The Iranian Communist Party, now banned and persecuted in that country.

Turkmen   A people of Turkic origin living in northwest Afghanistan and across the border in the Soviet Union.

Uzbegs   People of north Afghanistan who provide many of the country's workers and businessmen, as well as (arguably) the world's best horsemen.

Index

Picture acknowledgments

The publishers would like to thank the following for the pictures reproduced
in this book: Associated Press 9, 11, 23, 51, 55, 58, 65, 69, 72; Camera Press
Ltd 8, 10, 16, 24, 25, 28, 37, 44, 45, 52–3, 59, 63, 73; Mary Evans Picture
Library 35; NAAS *cover*; Novosti 39, 56–7, 70; Popperfoto 18, 26, 43, 46,
61, 71 (large); The Mansell Collection 31, 32, 34; The Research House 20,
21, 40, 50, 54, 67; TOPHAM 12, 13, 14, 15, 22, 27, 29, 30, 36, 41, 42,
64, 66, 71 (inset). Artwork on pages 17, 49, 62 by Malcolm Walker.